TALKING BALLS!

Richard Foster is a freelance sportswriter and author. He has written for The Football League, Sabotage Times and The Set Pieces and has appeared on talkSPORT and BBC London. Foster is the author of *The A-Z of Football Hates: The Definitive Guide to Everything That is Rotten in the Beautiful Game* and *The Agony & The Ecstasy: A Comprehensive History of the Football League Play-Offs.*

First published by Carlton Books in 2015

Carlton Books
20 Mortimer Street
London W1T 3JW

Copyright © Carlton Books 2015

A CIP catalogue for this book is available from the British Library.

ISBN 978-1-78097-683-9

10 9 8 7 6 5 4 3 2 1

Printed and bound by CPI Group (UK) Ltd, Croydon, CR0 4YY

TALKING BALLS!

THE GREATEST AND FUNNIEST SPORTS QUOTES OF ALL TIME

Edited by Richard Foster

CARLTON
BOOKS

Contents

Introduction

Muhammad Ali, Brian Clough and Geoff Boycott were all at the very top of their game, rightly acknowledged as masters of their sport but much of their reputation was secured by what they said outside the ring or off the pitch. Their lasting legacy is so much more than just a record of sporting deeds.

Ali floored as many opponents out of the ring as in it. His withering put-downs of George Foreman in particular were as damaging as his lightning fast hands. My favourite Ali quote sums up his supreme confidence and the cool rationale behind it: "It's not bragging if you can back it up."

Clough was another one skilled in the art of keeping everyone else in his considerable shadow, but he could also be devastatingly funny, as with his comment on Roy Keane's disciplinary problems: "He's had more holidays than Judith Chalmers." Boycott's well-known bluntness is captured in his assessment of English cricket's *enfant terrible* Kevin Pietersen, when he insisted that there were "more brains in a pork pie."

Alongside the sharp, witty put-downs there is also plenty of room in this book for the blunt blunders. So numerous slip-ups and gaffes, which we can all enjoy at others' expense, are featured as well. Despite being an excellent broadcaster, David Coleman will always be remembered for his various cock-ups. His name has become enshrined in popular culture for those high profile errors, but he is not alone and there are many tripping over themselves in his wake. Welcome to *Talking Balls*.

Richard Foster

Football

As the biggest sport across the globe, football is forever in the spotlight with each wayward word and verbal volley captured. From Arsene to Zlatan, the very best and the worst are featured here.

Football

" He can't kick with his left foot, he can't head, he can't tackle, and he doesn't score that many goals. Apart from that, he's alright. "
George Best on David Beckham

" The average English footballer could not tell the difference between an attractive woman and a corner flag. "
Walter Zenga on English footballers

" Mourinho is the best coach in the world, but as a man he needs to learn manners and respect. "
Mario Balotelli lectures Mourinho on being civil

" In some ways, cramp is worse than having a broken leg. "
Kevin Keegan

" He covers every blade of grass, but that's only
because his first touch is crap. "
David Jones on Carlton Palmer

" If you expose the opposition's weaknesses enough,
then, in the end, those weaknesses will be exposed. "
Football manager Sam Allardyce

" Messi can do some amazing things, but anything
he can do, Joe Cole can do as well, if not better. "
Steven Gerrard

" I would not be bothered if we lost every
game as long as we won the World Cup. "
German footballer Michael Ballack

Football

" Someone said you could write Barry's knowledge of tactics on a stamp. You'd need to fold the stamp in half. "
Steve Claridge on Barry Fry

" And Bale slides the ball inside Cech. "
Football commentator John Motson

" You don't need balls to play in a cup final. "
Steve Claridge with an anatomical revelation

" Martin O'Neill, standing, hands on hips, stroking his chin. "
BBC football commentator Mike Ingham

" One accusation you can't throw at me is that I've always done my best. "
Footballer Alan Shearer

" This will be their 19th consecutive game without a win unless they can get an equalizer. "
BBC football commentator Alan Green

" He's like my missus – telepathic! Just like her, he always knew which buttons to press. "
Andy Cole on Alex Ferguson

" He's like a second wife. "
Benni McCarthy on striking relationship with Jason Roberts

" We will wait for him like a good wife waiting for her husband who is in jail. "
Jurgen Klopp shows patience with Mats Hummels' return from injury

Football

" That David Seaman is a handsome young man but he spends too much time looking in his mirror rather than at the ball. "
Brian Clough on David Seaman

" I think Pat's dress sense is dreadful. I would like to see him in a nice shirt or a proper tie. "
Mary Nevin on son Pat's sartorial sense – or not

" Ed De Goey is the worst-dressed man I've ever seen. One pair of jeans, one pair of trainers, one shirt and one haircut. "
John Terry on teammate and keeper

" You can punch someone, you can go over the top and break someone's leg, which is unnecessary, in a tackle, but to go against team orders in the dressing room is terrible. "
Gary Neville's questionable morality over Kevin Mirallas' penalty miss

" We lost because we didn't win. "
Sweden football manager Lars Lagerback

" I've got nothing against foreign managers, they are very nice people. Apart from Arsene Wenger. "
Tony Pulis getting personal

" To get players to come to Plymouth
I had to beat them up and drug them. "
**Ian Holloway on unusual recruitment
tactics in the South West**

" If that had gone in, it would have been a goal. "
David Coleman

" If God had wanted us to play football in
the clouds, he'd have put grass up there. "
Brian Clough

Football

" Neil Sullivan has stopped absolutely everything they have thrown at him… Wimbledon 1, Manchester United 1. "
Football commentator Mike Ingham

" Sir David Beckham? You're having a laugh. He's just a good footballer with a famous bird. Can you imagine if Posh was called Lady Beckham? We'd never hear the end of it. "
Ian Holloway on possible knighthood for Beckham

" You don't score 64 goals in 86 games without being able to score goals. "
BBC sports reporter Alan Green

" Every dog has its day, and today is woof day! Today I just want to bark. "
Ian Holloway's canine take on promotion

Football

" I love Blackpool. We're very similar.
We both look better in the dark. "
Ian Holloway on his affinity with Blackpool

" We ended the season on a high – apart
from the last game which we lost. "
David Beckham's positive mental attitude

" Everything's been really positive and smooth.
Apart from, obviously, the season. "
**David Beckham taking positive thinking
to a new level at LA Galaxy**

" I have no doubts whatsoever that Germany will
thrash England and qualify easily for the World
Cup. What could possibly go wrong? The English
haven't beaten us in Munich for 100 years. "
**Former German player Uli Hoeness on the
eve of Germany's 5-1 defeat to England**

" This chance is unmissable and well, er, he misses it! "
Alan Hansen

" If you score against the Italians you deserve a goal. "
Ron Atkinson

" I'm not saying we shouldn't have a foreign manager,
but I think he should definitely be English.
**Paul Merson making the case for an
English-speaking manager**

" I feel I have broken the ice with the English
people. In 60 days, I have gone from being
Volvo Man to Svensational. "
Sven-Goran Eriksson

" The ageless Dennis Wise, now in his 30s. "
Football commentator Martin Tyler

Football

" Gotze's leaving because he's Guardiola's favourite. If it's anyone's fault, it's mine. I can't make myself shorter and learn Spanish. "
Jurgen Klopp takes Mario Gotze's departure to Bayern Munich personally

" Thank you to the mothers who gave birth to these Atleti players…their sons have massive balls. "
Diego Simeone is clearly a mummy's boy, after they beat Chelsea in Champions League semi-final

" Romario punched me in the face from behind. You know what? I deserved it. "
Diego Simeone's brutal honesty

" He dribbles a lot and opposition doesn't like it – you can see it all over their faces. "
Ron Atkinson

" I'd love to be a mole on the wall in the
Liverpool dressing room at half-time."
Kevin Keegan

" We haven't had the rub of the dice."
Bobby Robson

" If someone comes in with a mobile phone, I'll
throw it in the North Sea. And we need lectures
about why we can't have everyday things like
mayonnaise, ketchup and Coke."
Paolo Di Canio sets down some rules

" I saw him in the tunnel and thought 'Christ,
it's Jack and the Beanstalk, this!'"
Alex Bruce sizing up Peter Crouch

" Footballers are no different from human beings."
Former England manager Graham Taylor

" McCarthy shakes his head in agreement
with the referee. "
Football commentator Martin Tyler

" One thing's for sure, a World Cup without
me is nothing to watch. "
**Zlatan Ibrahimovic on the global disappointment
over Sweden's failure to qualify**

" You can never beat Alex Ferguson and when
you do you come off second best. "
**Steve McClaren, Fergie's Number Two,
knows his place**

" It's the end-of-season curtain-raiser. "
Former Aston Villa striker Peter Withe

" It's getting tickly now – squeaky-bum time, I call it. "
**Sir Alex Ferguson on feeling the pressure
of a tight title race**

" I'd like to have seen Tony Morley left on as a down-and-out winger. "
Blackpool legend and football commentator Jimmy Armfield

" Anybody who is thinking of applying for the Scotland job in the next eight or nine years should go get themselves checked out by about 15 psychiatrists. "
Martin O'Neill airs his views on head coach

" So I'm a liar? He's thin then, that gives reason to call me a liar. "
Marco Materazzi lays it on thick in a spat with Rafa Benitez

" I have watched Barnsley and it is clear they are not Real Madrid. "
Roberto Mancini is clearly on his game

" Probably when Lionel Messi ran
straight past me. "
**David Beckham on realising it
was time to retire**

" What do you think they're smoking over
there at The Emirates? "
**Liverpool owner JW Henry is disparaging
about an Arsenal bid for Luis Suarez**

" …and their manager, Terry Neill, isn't here
today, which suggests he is elsewhere. "
Football commentator Brian Moore

" I'm not going to make it a target but it is
something to aim for. "
Ex-Manchester United star Steve Coppell

Football

" Jose was one of those guys on a surfboard who could stay longer on the wave than anyone else."
Alex Ferguson on surfer Mourinho

" Money isn't the most important thing. It is important, of course. I am not Mahatma Gandhi."
Jurgen Klopp on materialism

" Real possession football this. And Zico's lost it."
Football commentator John Helm

" Queen's Park against Forfar – you can't get more romantic than that."
Archie McPherson

" It's a game of two teams."
BBC football reporter Peter Brackley

Football

" Well, we got nine and you can't score more
than that. "
**Former England football manager
Bobby Robson**

" Maybe Louis does have a golden willy. "
Arjen Robben on Van Gaal's magic touch

" It was like something out of *Swan Lake*
– it's that blatant. "
Steve Bruce on Gary Cahill's balletic dive

" He's worse than Dracula, because at least
Dracula comes out of his coffin now
and then. "
**Bruce Grobbelaar gets his teeth
into Simon Mignolct**

" I am a firm believer that if you score one goal the other team have to score two to win. "
Howard Wilkinson

" Football's a game of skill; we kicked them a bit and they kicked us a bit. "
Former England football hard man
Graham Roberts

" Sometimes you want Obertan to open his legs and do something a bit exciting. "
Alan Pardew

" Mario Balotelli is like Marmite, you either love him or hate him. Me, I'm in between. "
Joe Royle

" White liquid in a bottle has to be milk. "
Rafa Benitez

" More chuffed than a badger at the start
of the mating season. "
**Ian Holloway expresses his joy
in black and white**

" For all his horses, knighthoods, or
championships, he hasn't got two of what
I've got. And I don't mean balls. "
**Brian Clough on the difference between
him and Alex Ferguson before he won his
second Champions League trophy**

" There's a one-man Liverpool wall, hurriedly
put together. "
Football commentator John Murray

" There are a whole lot of teams in the
bottom six this season. "
Graeme Le Saux

" We had already beaten them 4-0 and 7-0 earlier this season, so we knew we were in for a really tough game today."
Barry Ferguson never underestimates his opponents

" Viv Anderson has pissed a fatness test."
John Helm aka Mrs Malaprop

" Maths is totally done differently to what I was teached when I was at school."
David Beckham

" I'd love the person who taught Jose Mourinho English to taught me."
So do we Steve Claridge, so do we

" With Harry [Redknapp], two plus two makes five, not three."
Milan Mandaric sums it up

Football

" Argentina won't be at Euro 2000 because
they are from South America. "
**Kevin Keegan's logic is as strong as his
geography**

" Football's like a big market place and people go to
the market every day to buy their vegetables. "
Bobby Robson's low opinion of footballers

" Chris Waddle is off the pitch at the moment –
exactly the position he is at his most menacing. "
Gerald Sinstadt

" I'd like to think it's a case of crossing the
i's and dotting the t's. "
Former manager Dave Bassett

Football

" I never predict anything and I never will do."
Footballer Paul Gascoigne

" If someone in the crowd spits at you, you have just got to swallow it."
Gary Lineker

" We'll not give up even if we're 12 points behind with one game left."
Joe Hart whose spirit is stronger than his maths

" If you just need a first eleven and four others, why did Columbus sail to India to discover America?"
Claudio Ranieri poses the question we all want to know

" Kicked wide of the goal with such precision."
Football presenter Des Lynam

Football

" They're the second-best team in the world and there's no higher praise than that. "
Kevin Keegan

" Chips without mayonnaise is not chips. "
Ronald Koeman

" We have to score more goals than we concede to win a game of football. "
Sam Allardyce, master tactician

" I'm not going to pick out anyone in particular, but Jay-Jay Okocha should not be captain of a football club. "
Former footballer Rodney Marsh

" I saw him kick the bucket over there which suggests he's not going to be able to continue. "
Football pundit Trevor Brooking

Football

" That's football, Mike. Northern Ireland have had
several chances and haven't scored but England
had no chances and scored twice. "
Trevor Brooking

" Goodnight, and don't forget to put your cocks back. "
Football pundit Jimmy Hill

" And there's Ray Clemence looking as
cool as ever out in the cold. "
Jimmy Hill

" I've told the players we need to win so that
I can have the cash to buy some new ones. "
Football manager Chris Turner

" Money has never won anything. "
Profound from Petr Cech – and maybe hypocritical

Football

" How can you replace Fergie's record? You could live
to be one million years old and not see it surpassed. "
Tommy Docherty goes long on longevity

" I've eaten a bar of soap before and then
I swear like a trooper. "
Ian Holloway cleans up his act

" He had an eternity to play that ball...
but he took too long over it. "
Football commentator Martin Tyler

" I'm very excited to see him in the flesh
and play with him. "
**Theo Walcott may be getting too
excited about Ozil's arrival**

" If you want, you can make a silence very noisy.
You could make noise with my silence. "
The enigmatic Jose Mourinho

" I never comment on referees and I'm not going to break the habit of a lifetime for that prat."
Ron Atkinson

" Peter Reid is hobbling, and I've got a feeling that will slow him down."
Football commentator John Motson

" The weather was good, everything was great. Only the result was shit."
Jurgen Klopp on 2013 Champions League Final

" Last year I ate beef, now I have chicken but I'm still really hungry."
David Luiz on his appetite for more titles

" It's a lovely ice cream that has been melting in the sun for the last 16 months."
Guillem Balague sums up Barcelona's humbling defeat to Bayern Munich

" I've never had a big head. I do not consider
myself to be the best in the world, nor the worst.
I am me and that is enough. "
Mario Balotelli

" I've got a plan to stop him, it's called
a machete. Plan B is a machine gun! "
**Sir Alex Ferguson on how to
counter Ronaldo**

" I'll probably open a bottle of champagne tonight...
I might even treat myself to a bag of crisps. "
Neil Warnock

" I was recognised too much and sometimes
women would suddenly climb all over me. "
Marouane Fellaini

Football

" Sergio Ramos is a fantastic football player,
but he is not a doctor."
Jose Mourinho

" You've got to miss them to score sometimes."
Football manager Dave Bassett

" Unfortunately, we keep kicking ourselves in
the foot."
Ray Wilkins

" The most vulnerable area for goalies
is between their legs..."
Football commentator Andy Gray

" Brazil – they're so good it's like they are running
around the pitch playing with themselves."
Football commentator John Motson

" Coaches are like watermelons."
Massimo Cellino

" I use the word embarrassing because I'm
trying to be respectful."
Gus Poyet after 8-0 defeat to Southampton

" Alex McLeish and I even competed for the
acne cream when we were younger. Obviously,
I won that one."
Gordon Strachan is spot on

" I tried to get the disappointment out of my
system by going for a walk. I ended up 17 miles
from home and I had to phone my wife Lesley
to come and pick me up."
Gordon Strachan

Football

" I come first, not football. "
Cristiano Ronaldo

" If that was a penalty, we should be
playing basketball. "
Niko Kovac, Croatian manager

" He was old a year ago, now he's young. "
Gary Neville on Ryan Giggs aka Peter Pan

" The best way to win games is to score goals. "
Manuel Pellegrini on tactical nuances

" It's like having a choice between two blokes
to nick your wife. "
Gary Neville's take on Hobson's choice

Football

" If history is going to repeat itself I should think we can expect the same thing again. "
Terry Venables

" I'm not a believer in luck... but I do believe you need it. "
Former England footballer Alan Ball

" Congratulations to him, he's got the chance to wave his fingers at a few more managers in this competition. "
Tim Sherwood on Benfica boss Jorge Jesus

" The lad got overexcited when he saw the whites of the goalpost's eyes. "
Steve Coppell

" Newcastle, of course, unbeaten in their
last five wins. "
Brian Moore

" They are men. I'm a manager, not a babysitter. "
**Tim Sherwood – not keen on his own
players either**

" Mark Hughes at his very best: he loves
to feel people right behind him. "
Kevin Keegan

" I'm going to make a prediction; it could
go either way. "
Ron Atkinson

" Some people are frustrated with that result?
Some people can **** off. "
Mick McCarthy

" This is football from the 19th century. The only thing I can bring more to win was a Black & Decker to destroy the wall. "
Jose Mourinho on West Ham United's Victorian approach

" I couldn't give a ****. Good old Jose, moaning again. "
Sam Allardyce unimpressed by Mourinho's 19th century dig

" It's not helpful when the three fountains of knowledge on *Match of the Day* make a mountain out of a molehill. "
Nigel Pearson

" My parents have been there for me, ever since I was about seven. "
David Beckham

" He was a quiet man, Eric Cantona, but
he was a man of few words. "
David Beckham

" I said to my players I was squeezing my ass but it
was the wrong expression. I have twitched my ass
on the bench because we were out of balance. "
Louis Van Gaal

" Football's not just physical, it's menthol too. "
Football manager Phil Brown

" Benitez took the elephant in the room
and put it on the table. "
Gareth Southgate

" I don't want Rooney to leave these shores
but if he does, I think he'll go abroad. "
Ian Wright

" Stokes gets a straight yellow for that challenge."
Ronnie Whelan

" Arsenal literally finished the game after
15 minutes."
Former Arsenal striker Ian Wright

" If you don't give Martinez a chance,
what chance has he got?"
Paul Merson

" I've served more time than Ronnie Biggs
did for the Great Train Robbery."
Malcolm Allison on touchline ban

" Liverpool will be without Kvarme tonight
– he's illegible."
Jimmy Armfield

" Devon Loch was a better finisher. "
Ron Atkinson on Carlton Palmer

" Great teams always have a Plan B. Look at
Barcelona. Their Plan B is to stick to Plan A. "
Pundit Johnny Giles

Jimmy Hill: Don't sit on the fence, Terry,
what chance do you think Germany has
got of getting through?
Terry Venables: I think it's 50-50.

" There's nobody fitter at his age, except
maybe Raquel Welch. "
Ron Atkinson on 39 year-old Gordon Strachan

" It's nice for us to have a fresh face in the
camp to bounce things off. "
Lawrie Sanchez

" They didn't change positions, they just
moved the players around. "
Terry Venables

" I know where the linesman should've stuck his
flag, and he would have had plenty of help. "
Ron Atkinson

" If that was a penalty I'll plait sawdust. "
Ron Atkinson

" The Sheffield United strip looks as if it
was designed by Julian Clary when he
had a migraine. "
Sean Bean

" I used to go missing a lot – Miss Canada,
Miss United Kingdom, Miss Germany. "
George Best

" Liverpool are my nap selection – I prefer to sleep when they're on the box. "
Stan Bowles

" Michael Owen – he's got the legs of a salmon. "
Craig Brown

" If Glenn Hoddle said one word to his team at half-time, it was concentration and focus. "
Ron Atkinson

" I think that was a moment of cool panic there. "
Ron Atkinson

" I would not say he [David Ginola] is the best left winger in the Premiership, but there are none better. "
Ron Atkinson

" This is the first time Denmark has ever reached the World Cup Finals, so this is the most significant moment in Danish history. "
Football commentator John Helm

" And I honestly believe we can go all the way to Wembley – unless somebody knocks us out. "
Dave Bassett

" At Rangers I was third choice left back – behind an amputee and a Catholic. "
Craig Brown

" Footballers' wives should be seen and not heard. "
Tony Waiters

" This is an unusual Scotland side because they have good players. "
Javier Clemente, Spanish coach

Football

"He's had more holidays than Judith Chalmers."
Brian Clough on Roy Keane's long line of suspensions

" Ally MacLeod thinks tactics are a new kind of mint."
Billy Connolly

" Atillio Lombardo is starting to pick up a bit of English on the training ground. The first word he learned was 'wanker'."
Steve Coppell

" I felt sorry for the match ball – it came off the pitch crying."
Johann Cruyff

" Doug Ellis said he was right behind me. I told him I'd sooner have him in front of me where I could see him."
Tommy Docherty

" Most people who can remember when (Notts) County were a great club are dead. "
Jack Dunnett

" One Wigan director wanted us to sign Salford Van Hire because he thought he was a Dutch international. "
Fred Eyre

" Nicky Butt's a real Manchester boy. He comes from Gorton where it is said they take the pavements in of a night time. "
Alex Ferguson

" I still believe we have an outside chance of reaching the Play-Offs, but then again, I believe in Father Christmas. "
Trevor Francis

Football

" I was delighted to get a point. Normally the only thing we get out of London is the train from Euston."
Jimmy Frizzell, Oldham manager

" Hugo Sanchez is a very dangerous man. He is about as welcome as a piranha in a bidet."
Jesus Gil

" The first thing I read now in *The Telegraph* is the obituaries. If I'm not in it, I have a good day."
Jack Hayward

" We are down to the barest knuckle."
Glenn Hoddle

" The biggest problem I've got down here in Plymouth is seagulls shitting on my car."
Ian Holloway

" Only God knows …You're talking to him now. "
Zlatan Ibrahimovic

" Ian Rush unleashed his left foot and it hit
the back of the net. "
Mike England

" Wilkins sends an inch-perfect pass to no
one in particular. "
Bryon Butler

" The World Cup – truly an international event. "
Football commentator John Motson

" If you can't stand the heat in the dressing room,
get out of the kitchen. "
Terry Venables

Football

" For those of you watching in black and white,
Spurs are playing in yellow. "
Football commentator John Motson

" I sent myself off. It's impossible to be more
embarrassed than that. There was nothing more
I could do so I went to the dressing room. "
**Phil Scolari's novel way of dealing with
defeat at Gremio**

" When I sleep too much I don't score.
That's the reason I go out a lot. "
Romario on his unusual training regime

" Neymar is the Justin Bieber of football. Brilliant
on the old YouTube. Cat piss in reality. "
Joey Barton

" It was like seducing the most beautiful woman in the world. Then failing on the moment for which you did it all."
Socrates on disappointment of Brazil's 1982 World Cup exit

" Some people tell me that we professional players are slaves. Well, if this is slavery, give me a life sentence."
Bobby Charlton

" Playing against a defensive opposition is just as bad as making love to a tree."
Jorge Valdano

" It was a game of two halves and we were rubbish in both of them."
Brian Horton

" His weakness is that he doesn't think he has any."
Arsene Wenger on Alex Ferguson

" The highest educated person at Real Madrid is the woman cleaning the toilets."
Joan Gaspart, Barcelona president

" There are only three things that stand still in the air: a hummingbird, a helicopter and Dada."
Brazilian footballer Dada Maravilha

" Those who tell you it's tough at the top have never been at the bottom."
Joe Harvey

" I know more about football than politics."
Harold Wilson

" If Stan Bowles could pass a betting shop like he can pass a ball he'd have no worries at all. "
Ernie Tagg, Crewe manager

" Both teams were feeling each other in the first half. "
John Terry goes a bit tactile over Chelsea's match against PSG

" I tell you what, that's a great tackle... Actually it's a foul, no doubt about it. I can't believe the ref has let him get away with that. "
Robbie Savage proving he can argue with himself

" I can't help but laugh at how perfect I am. "
Zlatan Ibrahimovic

" Belgium is not a hotpot of international football. "
Alan Brazil

" They gave the Serbian FA a poultry fine. "
Alan Brazil feels the authorities are a little bit chicken

" Some players need a boot up the backside. Other players need the arm. "
Alan Brazil

" It's real end-to-end stuff, but unfortunately it's all up at Forest's end. "
Chris Kamara gets a bit dizzy

" Statistics are there to be broken. "
Chris Kamara

" Manchester City are defending like beavers. "
Chris Kamara

" If you're chopping and changing the team you don't get that word I can't pronounce beginning with 'C'. "
Paul Merson

" People just looked lost. Too many players looked like fish on trees. "
Paul Merson

" I'm feeling a lot of pressure with the swan in Scotland. It's not far and I'm more scared of the swan than of football. What's football compared to life? A swan with bird flu, for me that's a drama. "
Jose Mourinho on bird flu

" If the club decide to sack me because of bad results that's part of the game. If it happens I will be a millionaire and get another club a couple of months later. "
Jose Mourinho does not seem too worried

" If Chelsea are naïve and pure then
I'm Little Red Riding Hood. "
Rafa Benitez's fairy tale

" He makes you feel 25-foot tall and I'm
going to sorely miss him. "
**Ian Holloway on Mourinho being s
acked by Chelsea**

" I've been consistent in patches this season. "
Theo Walcott

" It was goalposts for jumpers. "
Tony Mowbray mixing up his analogy

" I think one of these teams could win this. "
**Andy Townsend accurately predicts UEFA
Super Cup Final**

Football

" Javier Pastore wouldn't get a beach ball off
me if we were locked in a phone box. "
Joey Barton

" I can't protect people who don't want to run and
train, and are about three stone overweight. "
**Harry Redknapp not being very protective
about Adel Taarabt**

" If you don't know the answer to that question
then I think you are an ostrich. Your head
must be in the sand. "
**Nigel Pearson in a spat with Ian Baker,
a local journalist**

" What Carew does with a football, I can do
with an orange. "
Zlatan Ibrahimovic

Football

" You bought a Ferrari but you drive it like a Fiat. "
Ibrahimovic on his career at Barcelona

" I like fireworks too, but I set them off in gardens or kebab stands. I never set fire to my own house. "
Ibrahimovic distances himself from Mario Balotelli

" I managed lots of clubs. I had more clubs than Jack Nicholson. "
Bobby Gould

" Aaron Ramsey hasn't always been the flavour of the Arsenal fans' eyes. "
Craig Burley

" It can only happen in football – it's the Rocky Balboa scenario. "
Alvin Martin

" It's a real day for Nigel Adkins today, really."
Martin Keown gets real

" Whatever happened to Dagenham and Redgrave?"
Alan Brazil

" What I saw in Holland and Germany was
that the majority of people are Dutch in Holland
and German in Germany."
Peter Taylor on Europe

" Manchester City are built on sand and I don't
mean that because their owners are from the Arab
countries."
Kevin Keegan

" The aura of uninvincibility has gone,
if there is such a word."
Adrian Chiles

Football

" I can see the carrot at the end of the tunnel. "
Stuart Pearce on his unusual vision

" I'd like to play for an Italian club, like Barcelona. "
Mark Draper

" Running is for animals. You need a brain and a
ball for football. "
Louis Van Gaal

" Van Gaal is a dictator, with no sense of humour. "
Ibrahimovic

" It was nice to hear Ray Wilkins speaking
so articulate. "
Micky Quinn

" I've watched the replay and there is absolutely no doubt: it's inconclusive. "
Garth Crooks

" Hopefully Andy (Carroll) has only tweeted his hamstring. "
Sam Allardyce

" Have Liverpool done too much tinkering and tailoring with their system? "
Stan Collymore

" At Chelsea, a sacking is just another day at the office. "
Andre Villas-Boas

" I like Balotelli: he's even crazier than me. He can score a winner, then set fire to the hotel. "
Ibrahimovic praises Balotelli

" The minute's silence was immaculate, I have never heard a minute's silence like that. "
Glenn Hoddle

" The world looks a totally different place after two wins. I can even enjoy watching *Blind Date* or laugh at *Noel's House Party*. "
Gordon Strachan

" I was surprised, but I always say nothing surprises me in football. "
Les Ferdinand

" One or two bad eggs have spoiled it. If it had been done my way, they would have been out of the building straight away. "
Joey Barton

" A football team is like a piano. You need eight men to carry it and three who can play the damn thing. "
Bill Shankly

" There was nothing wrong with the timing, he was just a bit late. "
Mark Bright

" A boy from Croxteth should not use hair product. "
Jamie Carragher on Wayne Rooney

" All I really want is for Crystal Palace to win every game between now and the end of time. "
Eddie Izzard on becoming a director of the club

Athletics

For some unknown reason athletics attracts its fair share of commentary calamities and bitchy backbiting, so whether it be track or field there is always somebody putting their foot in it.

Athletics

" In a moment we hope to see the pole vault over the satellite. "
David Coleman has high expectations

" She's dragged the javelin back into the twentieth century. "
Ron Pickering

" One of the great unknown champions because very little is known about him. "
David Coleman

" He's got to stick the boot in, to use a technical term. "
Athlete Steve Ovett

" I am still looking for shoes that will make running on streets seem like running barefoot across the bosoms of maidens. "
Dave Bronson, US marathon runner

Athletics

" What will my country give me if I win
100 metres gold in Sydney? Tobago probably. "
Ato Boldon, Trinidad and Tobago sprinter

" I don't think the discus will generate any
interest until they let us start throwing
them at one another. "
Al Oerter

" The late start is due to the time. "
David Coleman

" That's the fastest time ever run
– but it's not as fast as the world record. "
David Coleman

" Behind every good decathlete,
there's a good doctor. "
Bill Toomey

Athletics

" Seb Coe is a Yorkshireman. So he's a complete
bastard and will do well in politics."
Daley Thompson

" Italian men and Russian women
do not shave before a race."
Eddie Ottoz, Italian athlete

" The decathlon is nine Mickey Mouse events and
the 1500 metres."
Steve Ovett

" When I lost my decathlon world record
I took it like a man. I only cried for ten hours."
Daley Thompson

" She's not Ben Johnson, but then who is?"
David Coleman

" A very powerful set of lungs, very much hidden by that chest of his. "
Athlete Alan Pascoe

" Running for money doesn't make you run fast. It makes you run first. "
Ben Jipcho, Kenyan athlete

" The best moment since I caught my tit in a mangle. "
Daley Thompson on winning Olympic gold in 1984

" Henry Rono, the man with those tremendous asbestos lungs. "
Ron Pickering

" He's a well balanced athlete; he has a chip on both shoulders. "
Derek Redmond on Linford Christie

" Being a decathlete is like having ten girlfriends. You have to love them all, and you can't afford losing one. "
Daley Thompson

" He is going up and down like a metronome. "
Ron Pickering

" There is Brendan Foster, by himself with 20,000 people. "
David Coleman

" And the hush of anticipation is rising to a crescendo. "
Ron Pickering

" I'm absolutely thrilled and over the world about it. "
Athlete Tessa Sanderson

Athletics

" ...and finally she tastes the sweet smell of success. "
Ian Edwards

" I know I'm no Kim Basinger, but she can't throw a javelin. "
Fatima Whitbread

" Watch the time. It gives you an indication of how fast they are running. "
Ron Pickering

" The British team need to pull their socks out. "
Steve Cram

" Any press is good press. So keep on ragging me. "
Carl Lewis throws down a challenge

" I started running in high school. I found out if you can run fast then you can get girls."
Kim Collins

" I became a great runner because if you're a kid in Leeds and your name is Sebastian you've got to become a great runner."
Lord Coe

" World records are only borrowed."
Lord Coe

" When you go into an indoors championship like this, it's different to the outdoors."
Athletics coach Max Jones

" It's a great advantage to be able to hurdle with both legs."
David Coleman

" Running is a lot like life. Only 10% is exciting. 90% of it is slog and drudge. "
David Bedford

" First is first, and second is nowhere. "
Ian Stewart

" You have to forget your last marathon before you try another. Your mind can't know what's coming. "
Frank Shorter, US marathon runner

" Ingrid Kristiansen, then, has smashed the world record, running the 5,000 metres in 14:58.89. Truly amazing. Incidentally, this is a personal best for Ingrid Kristiansen. "
David Coleman

" Life is about timing. "
Carl Lewis

Boxing

Boxers can deliver as many knock-out blows with their tongues as with their fists. With the action outside the ring being as intense as that inside, it's seconds out.

Boxing

" George Foreman is so ugly he should donate his face to the US Bureau of Wildlife. "
Muhammad Ali

" It's just a job. Grass grows, birds fly, waves pound the sand. I beat people up. "
Muhammad Ali

" I'm so fast that last night I turned off the light switch in my hotel room and was in bed before the room was dark. "
Muhammad Ali

" I'm going to fade into Bolivian. "
Former heavyweight champion Mike Tyson

" You can sum up this sport in two words: 'You never know.' "
Veteran boxing trainer Lou Duva

Boxing

" I've seen George Foreman shadow boxing
and the shadow won. "
Muhammad Ali

" There's a cliché in boxing – records are only for DJs. "
Dereck Chisora's coach Don Charles on records

" Well a tiger does not lose sleep over the
opinion of a sheep. "
**Carl Froch does not worry about
rival Adonis Stevenson**

" I sometimes feel like I'm the Miley Cyrus
of heavyweight boxing – young crazy super
sexy & don't give a ****. "
Tyson Fury

Boxing

" I truly believe that the confidence I have is
unbelievable. "
Prince Naseem Hamed

" Sure there have been injuries and deaths in boxing
– but none of them serious. "
Former champion Alan Minter

" He's a guy who gets up at 6 a.m. regardless
of what time it is. "
Veteran boxing trainer Lou Duva

" My mum says I used to fight my way out of the
cot. But I can't remember. That was before my
time. "
Former heavyweight champion Frank Bruno

" I'm only a prawn in the game. "
British boxer Brian London

" The British Press hate a winner who's British. They don't like any British man to have balls as big as a cow's, like I have. "
Nigel Benn

" Do I believe in superstitions? No. If you have superstitions, that's bad luck. "
Canadian middleweight Eric Lucas

" I quit school in the sixth grade because of pneumonia. Not because I had it, but because I couldn't spell it. "
Rocky Graziano

" Not being born to parents who were accountants was probably my biggest mistake. "
Chris Eubank

Boxing

" For ageing boxers, first your legs go. Then your reflexes go. Third your friends go. "
Willie Pep

" Boxing is like jazz. The better it is, the less people appreciate it. "
George Foreman

" No I don't mind the fight being at three in the morning. Everyone in Glasgow fights at three in the morning. "
Jim Watt

" All fighters are prostitutes and all promoters are pimps. "
Larry Holmes

Boxing

" It's not bragging if you can back it up."
Muhammad Ali

" He's standing there making a sitting target of himself."
Terry Lawless

" The chances of a rematch for Lewis are slim and none. And slim is out of town."
Don King

" To me, boxing is like ballet except there's no music, no choreography and the dancers hit each other."
Jack Handey

Boxing

" We'll have to take it on the chin. It's a
real body blow. "
British promoter Barry Hearn

" So over to the ringside – Harry Commentator is
your carpenter. "
BBC announcer

" If you even dream of beating me you'd better
wake up and apologise. "
Muhammad Ali

" There's more to boxing than hitting. There's
not getting hit, for instance. "
George Foreman hits the nail on the head

Boxing

" Chris Eubank is as genuine as a three dollar bill. "
Mickey Duff

" I want to rip out his heart and feed it to him.
I want to kill people. I want to rip their stomachs
out and eat their children. "
Mike Tyson

" The three toughest fighters I've ever been
up against were Sugar Ray Robinson, Sugar
Ray Robinson, and Sugar Ray Robinson.
I fought Sugar so many times, I'm surprized
I'm not diabetic! "
Jake LaMotta

Golf

From the first tee to the nineteenth hole, golf is littered with some of the most bizarre comments. Strip away the veneer of polite etiquette and the gloves are certainly off. Fore!

Golf

" It's a funny old game. One day you're a statue,
the next you're a pigeon. "
Peter Alliss

" Nick Faldo is as much fun as Saddam Hussein. "
Scott Hoch

" And now to hole eight, which is in fact
the eighth hole. "
Peter Alliss

" I made the last putt. It just didn't go in. "
Golfer Tom Kite

" I could have chosen a better word. If I had gone
for lousy, that might have captured it better. "
**Faldo digging a hole over his comments
about Sergio Garcia**

Golf

" That beautiful woman lives with me.
A rottweiler with lip-gloss."
Peter Alliss

" I disappeared down to the beach
after the Masters and lay on the
beach and cried."
**Greg Norman on accepting
defeat manfully**

" I owe a lot to my parents, especially my
mother and father."
Golf legend Greg Norman

" I think Steve is the nicest guy in
the world, too, so it couldn't happen
to a nicer guy."
Luke Donald on Steve Stricker

Golf

" Unfortunately the guys this afternoon will struggle
with a few pin positions. Eighth hole is a joke,
18th needs a windmill and a clown face. "
Ian Poulter goes crazy

" We have had our behinds handed to us for seven
of the last nine. That did not sit well with me. "
**Tom Watson gets to the bottom of why he took
on Ryder Cup captaincy**

" I try not to take anything now apart from
Corona and vodka. "
Lee Westwood

" It was my mum's birthday yesterday and
I wanted to win it for her because I forgot
to get her a present. "
George Coetzee

Golf

" He used to be fairly indecisive, but now he's
not so certain."
Peter Alliss

" Difficult couple of holes here – 15, 16 and 17."
Former golfer Howard Clark

" I feel like punching myself."
Rory McIlroy

" If you are caught on a golf course during a storm
and are afraid of lightning, hold up a 1-iron.
Not even God can hit a 1-iron."
Lee Trevino

" Ballesteros felt much better today after a 69."
Golf commentator Renton Laidlaw

" 'What do I think of Tiger Woods?' I don't know.
I never played there. "
Golfer Sandy Lyle

" I'm not saying my golf game went bad, but
if I grew tomatoes they'd come up sliced. "
Lee Trevino

" We've had it easy. When it blows here [St.
Andrews] even the seagulls walk. "
Nick Faldo

" When Seve gets his Porsche going, not even
San Pedro in heaven could stop him. "
**Jose Maria Olazabal on the
unstoppable Ballesteros**

Golf

" The only thing a golfer needs is more daylight. "
Ben Hogan

" We're going to have to start giving the Americans handicap strokes. This is getting boring. "
Sandy Lyle after another European Ryder Cup victory in 2006

" If you'd offered me a 69 at the start this morning I'd have been all over you. "
Golfer Sam Torrance

" Azinger is wearing an all-black outfit: black jumper, blue trousers, white shoes and a pink tea-cosy hat. "
Renton Laidlaw

Golf

" I can tell you now that I'll know exactly when
I want to retire; but when I reach that time
I may not know. "
Jack Nicklaus

" I played so good, it was like the hole
kept getting in the way of my ball. "
Calvin Peete

" They call it golf because all the other
four-letter words were taken. "
Raymond Floyd

" Like an octopus falling out of a tree. "
David Feherty on Jim Furyk's swing

Golf

" I don't like golf. It's not for me, it's too quiet. "
Mario Balotelli

" You can make a lot of money in this game. Just ask my ex-wives. Both of them are so rich that neither of their husbands work. "
Lee Trevino

" One of the reasons Arnie Palmer is playing so well is that, before each final round, his wife takes out his balls and kisses them. Oh my God, what have I just said. "
US Open TV commentator

Cricket

From brutal sledging out in the middle to the wit and wisdom up in the commentary box, cricket has many sides. Combining the risqué with the odd blunder it is truly a rich "seam" of content.

Cricket

" The only time an Australian walks is when his car runs out of petrol. "
Barry Richards

" I remember the 1992 World Cup final. It's my earliest memory. Inzamam-ul-Haq was skinny. Well, skinny-ish. "
Moeen Ali's fond memories of Inzamam-ul-Haq

" He played a cut so late as to be positively posthumous. "
John Arlott

" Gatting at fine leg – that's a contradiction in terms. "
Richie Benaud

Cricket

" How can you tell your wife you are just
popping out to play a match and then
not come back for five days?"
Rafa Benitez on the finer points of cricket

" I can't really say I'm batting badly. I'm not
batting long enough to be batting badly."
Greg Chappell

" Bill Frindall needs a small ruler. How about the
Sultan of Brunei? I hear he's only four foot ten."
Brian Johnston

" There were congratulations and high sixes
all round."
Richie Benaud

" I have prepared for the worst-case scenario, but it could be even worse than that. "
England spin bowler Monty Panesar

" If this bloke's a Test Match bowler, then my backside is a fire engine. "
David Lloyd on Kiwi, Nathan Astle, who took more than 50 Test Match wickets

" More brains in a pork pie. "
Geoff Boycott on Kevin Pietersen

" Ray Illingworth has just relieved himself at the Pavilion End. "
Brian Johnston

" You can't get out any earlier than the second ball of the game. "
David Lloyd

Cricket

" And we don't need a calculator to tell us
that the run-rate required is 4.5454 per over. "
Christopher Martin-Jenkins

" It is now possible they can get the impossible
score they first thought possible. "
CM-J on the art of the impossible

" He is a very dangerous bowler. Innocuous,
if you like. "
David Lloyd on Chris Harris

" It's never easy putting a rubber on,
is it Michael? "
**Jonathan Agnew poses a tricky one for
Michael Vaughan**

Cricket

" It was as if he [Cook] still writes to Santa
Claus and puts his tooth under his pillow
for the tooth fairy. "
Pietersen on Alastair Cook

" Get ready for a f****** broken arm. "
**Michael Clarke welcoming Jimmy Anderson to
the crease**

" England finally cruised to a 2-0 series win over
Bangladesh through the batting of Alastair
Cook, who hit a 12th Test century, and
Kevin Pietersen. "
BBC Sport report

" Brian Toss won the close. "
BBC cricket commentator Henry Blofeld

Cricket

" Admitting to being a Tory in Scotland is seen
as a bit weird like cross-dressing or liking cricket. "
Fraser Nelson, *The Spectator* editor

" I always walked... bit hard to stand there with
all three stumps lying on the ground. "
Glenn McGrath

" Punching lockers isn't the way forward for anyone.
There's only going to be one winner there. "
Ben Stokes

" There's only one head bigger than Tony Greig's
and that's Birkenhead. "
Fred Trueman

Cricket

" That slow-motion replay doesn't show how fast the ball was travelling. "
Richie Benaud

" Yes, he's a very good cricketer – pity he's not a better batter or bowler. "
Former England cricketer Tom Graveney

" Cricket is baseball on valium. "
Robin Williams

" I've done the elephant. I've done the poverty. I might as well go home. "
Phil Tufnell on Indian tour

Cricket

" Chris Lewis is the enigma with no variation. "
Vic Marks

" To dismiss this lad Denness you don't have
to bowl fast, you just have to run up fast. "
Brian Close

" Truly, I think I could get more runs if
England had some faster bowlers. "
Viv Richards

" And umpire Dickie Bird is gestating
wildly as usual. "
Tony Lewis

" Pakistan is the sort of place every man should
send his mother-in-law to, for a month,
all expenses paid. "
Ian Botham

Cricket

" On the first day, Logie decided to chance his arm
and it came off. "
Trevor Bailey

" You've got to make split-second decisions
so quickly. "
Geoffrey Boycott

" A very small crowd here today. I can count the
people on one hand. Can't be more than thirty. "
Michael Abrahamson

" I have never got to the bottom of streaking. "
Jonathan Agnew

" I don't think I've actually drunk a beer for
15 years, except a few Guinnesses in Dublin,
where it's the law. "
Ian Botham

Cricket

" A few years ago England would have struggled to beat the Eskimos."
Ian Botham

" The other advantage England have got when Phil Tufnell is bowling is that he isn't fielding."
Ian Chappell

" The only person who could be better than Brian Lara could be Brian Lara himself."
Colin Croft

" England have no McGrathish bowlers. There are hardly any McGrathish bowlers, except for [Glenn] McGrath."
Stuart Law

Cricket

" I can' bat, can't bowl and can't field these days.
I've every chance of being picked for England. "
Essex spinner Ray East

" I'm ugly, I'm overweight, but I'm happy. "
Andrew Flintoff

" I don't know an England player who
could fix a light bulb, let alone a match. "
Darren Gough

" Shane Warne's idea of a balanced diet is a
cheeseburger in each hand. "
Ian Healy

Cricket

" The blackcurrant jam tastes of fish to me. "
Derek Randall on caviar

" The third umpires should be changed as often
as nappies… and for the same reason. "
Navjot Sidhu

" I'd have looked even faster in colour. "
Fred Trueman

" As the ball gets softer it loses its hardness. "
Geoff Boycott

" I'm glad two sides of the cherry have
been put forward. "
Geoffrey Boycott

Cricket

" I'm a big believer that the coach is something you travel in to get to and from the game. "
Shane Warne, not a big fan of cricket coaching

" Geoff Boycott has the uncanny knack of being where fast bowlers aren't. "
Tony Greig

" They should cut Joel Garner off at the knees to make him bowl at a normal height. "
Geoff Boycott

" Unless something happens that we can't predict, I don't think a lot will happen. "
Fred Trueman

" It's a catch-21 situation. "
England batsman Kevin Pietersen

Cricket

" Life without sports is like life without underpants. "
Cricket umpire Billy Bowden gets to the naked truth

" I've been a bit of a useless tosser up to now. "
Paul Collingwood's self-awareness

" Pakistan without Ajmal is like ice-cream without chocolate topping. "
Ian Chappell

" He's nearly 34 – in fact he's 33. "
Richie Benaud

Cricket

" Pakistan can play well, but they have the ability to play badly, too."
Cricket commentator John Emburey

" Sorry, skipper, a leopard can't change its stripes."
Former Australian cricketer Lennie Pascoe

" We've won one on the trot."
Former England cricket captain Alec Stewart

" Like an elephant trying to do the pole vault."
Cricket commentator Jonathan Agnew on Inzaman-ul-Haq as the rotund Pakistan captain falls over his own stumps

" To stay in, you've got to not get out."
Cricket commentator Geoffrey Boycott

Cricket

" His tail is literally up!"
Cricket commentator Trevor Bailey

" Captaincy is 90% luck and 10% skill.
But don't try it without that 10%."
Cricket commentator Richie Benaud

" I sleep the whole day after breakfast to
get in shape for the game."
Chris Gayle

" I don't ask Kathy to face Michael
Holding. So I don't see why I should
be changing nappies."
Ian Botham on family duties

Cricket

" It's only a matter of time before the end
of this innings. "
Michael Peschardt

" Unless somebody can pull a miracle out of the fire,
Somerset are cruising into the semi-final. "
Fred Trueman

" Don't bother looking for that, let alone chasing it.
That's gone straight into the confectionery stall
and out again. "
Cricket commentator Richie Benaud

" And we have just heard, although this is not the
latest score from Bournemouth, that Hampshire
have beaten Nottinghamshire by nine wickets. "
Peter West

Cricket

" The umpire signals a bye with the air of a
weary stalk. "
Cricket commentator John Arlott

" Like an old lady poking with her umbrella
at a wasp's nest. "
**John Arlott on the batting style of
Australian Ernie Toshack**

" It's especially tense for Parker who's literally fighting
for a place on an overcrowded plane to India. "
Cricket commentator Trevor Bailey

" This is Cunis at the Vauxhall End. Cunis –
a funny sort of name. Neither one thing
nor the other. "
Alan Gibson

" Boycott, somewhat a creature of habit, likes exactly the sort of food he himself prefers. "
Dan Mosey

" The Port Elizabeth ground is more of a circle than an oval. It is long and square. "
Trevor Bailey

" Tavare has literally dropped anchor. "
Trevor Bailey

" A gun is no more dangerous than a cricket bat in the hands of a madman. "
Prince Phillip

Cricket

" He's not quite got hold of that one. If he had, it would have gone for nine "
Cricket commentator Richie Benaud on a Justin Langer six

" The first time you face up to a googly you're going to be in trouble if you've never faced one before. "
Trevor Bailey

" Clearly the West Indies are going to play their normal game, which is what they normally do. "
Tony Greig

" Welcome to Worcester where you've just missed seeing Barry Richards hitting one of Basil D'Oliveira's balls clean out of the ground. "
Brian Johnston

Cricket

" And Glenn McGrath dismissed for two, just 98 runs short of his century."
Richie Benaud

" There was a slight interruption there for athletics."
Richie Benaud on a streaker

" Well, Wally, I've been watching this game both visually and on TV."
Ken Barrington

" Andre Nel is big and raw-boned and I suspect he has the IQ of an empty swimming pool."
Adam Parore

" When there's a hosepipe ban covering three-quarters of the country, you don't expect a damp wicket at Lord's."
Bob Willis

Cricket

" This shirt is unique, there are only 200 of them. "
Richie Benaud

" Gavin Larsen is inexperienced in Test cricket in that this is his first Test. "
Geoff Boycott

" Denis Compton was the only player to call his partner for a run and wish him good luck at the same time. "
England cricketer John Warr

" Our Cheese was out there, growing runny in the heat. A Dairylea triangle thinking he was Brie. "
Kevin Pietersen on Matt Prior

Formula One

It is either the petrol fumes or watching the cars go round and round endlessly which makes racing commentators and drivers lose the plot and be so prone to verbal crashes.

" I don't make mistakes. I make prophecies which immediately turn out to be wrong. "
Murray Walker

" It's lap 26 of 58, which unless I'm very much mistaken, is half way. "
Murray Walker very much mistaken

" We need to get it up. I wish I could still get it up, but anyway. "
Bernie Ecclestone on... noise

" Do my eyes deceive me or is Senna's Lotus sounding rough? "
Formula One commentator Murray Walker

Formula One

" Mansell is slowing it down, taking it easy.
Oh no, he isn't! It's a lap record. "
Murray Walker

" The best classroom of all times was about
two car lengths behind Juan Manuel Fangio. "
Stirling Moss

" Brundle is driving an absolutely pluperfect race. "
Murray Walker is getting tense

" The battle is well and truly on if it wasn't
on before, and it certainly was. "
Murray Walker

" They make a female look low maintenance
these days, mate."
**Mark Webber on the complexities of
modern F1 car**

" The track is like a Tesco car park."
**Mark Webber not impressed with the new
Valencia circuit**

" This day is good for me. You are old now, so
hopefully it will be easier for me this year."
**Nico Rosberg wishes Lewis Hamilton a
happy 30th birthday**

" Your luck goes up and down like swings and
roundabouts."
Former world champion James Hunt

Formula One

" Alain Prost is in a commanding
second position. "
Murray Walker

" Jenson [Button] is literally putting his balls
on the line going up against Lewis. "
Formula One summariser David Coulthard

" Sometimes management is pissed off
with me because I tell them what's
going to happen. "
Niki Lauda

" I drove like a grandma from there to the end. "
Felipe Massa

Formula One

" It's getting dark, but that's partly because it's starting to get night. "
Damon Hill shedding light as a pundit

" In Spa I heard I had signed for £150m for three years. I was asking where the pen was but nobody came back to me! "
Sebastian Vettel

" The most important thing is that when we put on our helmets, we are all the same. "
Simona de Silvestro, female driver

" We now have exactly the same situation as we had at the start of the race, only exactly the opposite. "
Murray Walker

" Red Bull will be really worried about
the blue smoke coming from the back
of Mark Webber."
Martin Brundle

" That's history. I say history because
it happened in the past."
Murray Walker

" I kind of like to have someone looking
up my arse."
Mario Andretti

" Eddie Irvine is the Ian Paisley of Formula One."
Damon Hill

" My first priority is to finish above rather than below the ground. "
James Hunt

" Sure, I am one of the biggest stars in Finland. But we don't have that many. "
Kimi Raikkonen

" How has Formula One changed since my day? Less girls, more technology. "
Jody Scheckter

" If that's not a lap record, I'll eat the hat I don't normally wear. "
Murray Walker

Formula One

" What does it feel like being rammed
up the backside by Barrichello?"
Formula One commentator James Allen

" I've just stopped my startwatch."
Murray Walker

" Michael Schumacher would remain a formidable
challenge if he was driving a pram."
Frank Williams

" And now, excuse me while I interrupt myself."
Murray Walker

" You can cut the tension with a cricket stump."
Formula One commentator Murray Walker

Rugby
Union

In amongst the rucks and mauls, there are lots of slips and quips that squeeze through the scrum to give us plenty to rake over.

Rugby Union

" To play the game you have to play on the edge, but unfortunately he's gone to the edge of the cliff and jumped off it. "
Warren Gatland, British Lions coach, on Dylan Hartley's ban

" Sometimes you have to put your balls on the line. "
Gatland again, on dropping Brian O'Driscoll

" Sometimes you are unlucky. Sometimes you get what you deserve. And sometimes you get a kick in the nuts. "
Christian Day of Northampton

" Maybe it would help if I was a foot taller, had hair and didn't look like a pit bull. "
Richard Cockerill on self-image

" As long as my backside is pointing to the ground, Ewen McKenzie will not coach Australia. "
**An Australian rugby union official
clears up any doubt**

" Wales is not an easy country to coach because, basically, the Welsh are lazy. "
Ex-Scotland coach Jim Telfer

" It's only a thumb, I've got another one. "
Ryan Jones

" The way to get out of the poo is to fight with people who are prepared to get in the trenches with you. "
Brian Smith, London Irish coach

" You never want to be that guy who talks it up
and then can't back it up, training like Tarzan and
playing like Jane. "
James Haskell

" Basically I am like a dog – I just run after a ball. "
Chris Ashton

" The journo was as confused as a goldfish
with dementia. "
Nick Cummins, Australian player

" Last year we were all sizzle and steak, this year we had a
horror start but now we are off like a bride's nightie. "
Nick Cummins

" And there's Gregor Townsend's knee,
looking very disappointed. "
Gavin Hastings

Rugby Union

" Watching France at the moment is like watching clowns at the circus. "
Jeremy Guscott

" I don't know where Jonny Wilkinson is.
I do know where he is, he's not there. "
England hooker Brian Moore

" Pardon my French, but I thought we showed massive balls to go out there and play like that. "
Andy Farrell

" You can knock seven bells of **** out of each other and have a pint with him afterwards. "
Adam Jones on camaraderie

" Scotland may have to go to some dark places, but we'll bring some torches. "
Scott Johnson, coach

" Personally I wouldn't go there. You must get bored ****less in Newcastle. "
Louis Nicollin, Montpelier owner

" The knee doesn't trouble me when I'm walking, but it's painful when I kneel, like before my bank manager. "
David Leslie

" You don't like to see hookers going down on players like that. "
Murray Mexted

" The relationship between the Welsh and the English is based on trust and understanding. They don't trust us and we don't understand them. "
Dudley Wood, former RFU Secretary

Rugby Union

" Rugby is a good occasion for keeping thirty
bullies from the centre of the city."
Oscar Wilde

" Rafter again doing much of the unseen work
which the crowd relishes so much."
Rugby commentator Bill McLaren

" The ref's turned a blind ear."
**New Zealand rugby union commentator
Murray Mexted**

" A lot of these guys have waited a lifetime
not to win this."
Australian rugby union star David Campese

" If you can't take a punch you should play
table tennis."
Pierre Berbizier

Rugby Union

" Hopefully the rain will hold off for both sides. "
England player Lawrence Dallaglio

" I think you enjoy the game more if you don't know the rules. Anyway, you're on the same wavelength as the referees. "
Jonathan Davies

" The main difference between playing League and Union is that now I get my hangovers on Monday instead of Sunday. "
Tom David

Reporter: What of the future for Welsh rugby?
Welsh captain Mike Watkins: Over to the Angel for a lot of pints.

Rugby Union

" Scotland were victims of their own failure."
Gavin Hastings

" There's no such thing as a lack of confidence. You either have it or you don't."
England rugby international Rob Andrew

" I am not getting any younger and there are a few other guys in the same situation."
England's Nick Easter

" If you go out to get revenge on a team, you'll get bit on the arse."
Ireland player Sean O'Brien

Tennis

There have been some smashing moments from tennis players and commentators across the ages and here we serve up some real aces.

" I did play well in Australia. I don't know where you were. Were you under a rock?"
Roger Federer questioning a journalist

" The Gullikson twins here. An interesting pair, both from Wisconsin."
Dan Maskell

" Sure, I've been on the tube – I caught it to Eastbourne once."
Serena Williams

" As Boris Becker sits there, his eyes staring out in front of him, I wonder what he's thinking. I think he's thinking, 'I am Boris Becker.' At least I hope that's what he's thinking."
BBC Tennis commentator John Barrett

Tennis

" Lleyton Hewitt... his two greatest strengths are his legs, his speed, his agility and his competitiveness. "
Pat Cash doubles up

" Obviously, like Wembley is synonymous with tennis, snooker is synonymous with Sheffield. "
Richard Caborn, former Minister of Sport

" When Martina is tense it helps her relax. "
Dan Maskell

" Laura Robson... solid between the ears. "
Virginia Wade

" She changed coaches more times than I changed wives. "
The many times married Nick Bollettieri on Laura Robson

" The only thing that could have stopped Nadal this year is his knees."
Chris Wilkinson

" Nothing can prepare me for this. I just hope I play well and don't poop my pants."
Blaz Rola on facing Andy Murray

" It sucks."
Heather Watson unimpressed by her performance at the Australian Open

" Federer is human, but for how long?"
BBC tennis commentator

" Martina, she's got several layers of steel out there, like a cat with nine lives."
Wimbledon champion and BBC tennis commentator Virginia Wade

Tennis

" That shot he has to obliterate from
his mind a little bit. "
Mark Cox

" If someone says I'm not feminine, I say 'screw it.' "
Rosie Casals

" I call tennis the McDonalds of sport – you go in,
they make a quick buck out of you, and you're out. "
Pat Cash

" I still break racquets, but now I do it
in a positive way. "
Goran Ivanisevic

" Nobody likes me. And I couldn't care
a goddam stuff. "
Jimmy Connors

Tennis

" Getting your first serve in is a great way to avoid double faults. "
Former Australian tennis player John Fitzgerald

" It's quite clear that Virginia Wade is thriving on the pressure now that the pressure on her to do well is off. "
Harry Carpenter

" The trouble with me is that every match I play against five opponents: umpire, crowd, ball boys, court and myself. "
Goran Ivanisevic on his unequal struggle

" Whoever said, 'It's not whether you win or lose that counts,' probably lost. "
Martina Navratilova

" Time to remove every item of clothing and run through the streets of Glasgow."
Andy Murray gets swept away with Jamie Ward's Davis Cup victory

" I can cry like Roger, it's just a shame I can't play like him."
Andy Murray

" It'll certainly give the pigeons something to do."
Pat Cash on unveiling his own bust

" He can't cook."
Michael Chang on Pete Sampras's weaknesses

" I threw the kitchen sink at him but he went to the bathroom and got his tub."
Andy Roddick on losing to Roger Federer

American Football

The focus may be on getting
those crucial ten yards on the pitch
but the battle to win the war of
words is just as intense.

" My gluteus maximus is hurteus enormous. "
Tony Campbell

" My sister's expecting a baby, and I don't know if I'm going to be an uncle or an aunt. "
North Carolina State player Chuck Nevitt

" He treats us like men. He lets us wear earrings. "
Houston's Torrin Polk is so grateful to his coach

" A tie is like kissing your sister. "
Duffy Daugherty

" Coach Lombardi is very fair. He treats us all like dogs. "
Packers legend Henry Jordan

" If winning isn't everything, why do they keep score? "
Vince Lombardi

" Does Tom Landry smile? I don't know.
I only played there nine years. "
Walt Garrison

" I resigned as coach because of illness and fatigue.
The fans were sick and tired of me. "
John Ralston, Denver Broncos

" Most football players are temperamental.
That's 90% temper and 10% mental. "
Doug Plank

" On this team, we were all united in a
common goal: to keep my job. "
Lou Holtz, coach

American Football

" I've been big ever since I was little. "
William 'The Refrigerator' Perry

" What's the difference between a three week-old puppy and a sportswriter? In six weeks, the puppy stops whining. "
Mike Ditka, football coach

" The NFL, like life, is full of idiots. "
Randy Cross

" Defensively, I think it's important for us to tackle. "
Karl Mecklenburg

" The man who complains about the way the ball bounces is likely the one who dropped it. "
Lou Holtz

" Hey, the offensive linemen are the biggest guys on the field, they're bigger than everybody else, and that's what makes them the biggest guys on the field. "
John Madden

" I have two weapons; my arms, my legs and my brain. "
Michael Vick

" Sure, luck means a lot in football. Not having a good quarterback is bad luck. "
Don Shula

" I'm not allowed to comment on lousy officiating. "
Jim Finks

" I dunno. I never smoked any Astroturf. "
Joe Namath after being asked if he preferred grass or Astroturf

" If I drop dead tomorrow, at least I'll know I died in good health. "
Bum Phillips

" I want to rush for 1,000 or 1,500 yards. Whichever comes first. "
Running back George Rogers

" I never graduated college, but I was only there for two terms – Truman's and Eisenhower's. "
Alex Karras

" Emotion is highly overrated in football. My wife Corky is emotional as hell but can't play football worth a damn. "
John McKay

" If my mother put on a helmet and shoulder pads and a uniform that wasn't the same as the one I was wearing, I'd run over her if she was in my way. And I love my mother. "
Bo Jackson

" I may be dumb, but I'm not stupid. "
Terry Bradshaw

" Nobody in football should be called a genius. A genius is a guy like Norman Einstein. "
Joe Theismann

" People say I'll be drafted in the first round, maybe even higher. "
Craig Heyward

Baseball

Here are a few "strikes", the odd
home run and an occasional curveball
as we try to cover all the bases.

" I was thinking of making a comeback until I pulled a muscle vacuuming."
Johnny Bench

" It ain't the heat, it's the humility."
Yogi Berra

" When we [England] have a World Series, we ask other countries to participate."
John Cleese

" I watch a lot of baseball on the radio."
Gerald Ford, former US President

" Crowd? This isn't a crowd. It's a focus group!"
Fran Healy on disappointing turnout in Montreal

" Always go to other people's funerals;
otherwise they won't go to yours. "
Yogi Berra

" Baseball is 90 per cent mental. The other
half is physical. "
Yogi Berra has a maths problem

" I was glad to see Italy win. All the guys
on the team were Italians. "
Former Dodgers manager Tom Lasorda

" This is like deja vu all over again. "
Former New York Yankees player Yogi Berra

" Predictions are difficult. Especially
about the future. "
Yogi Berra

Baseball

" Any pitcher who throws at a batter and deliberately tries to hit him is a communist. "
Alvin Dark

" Philadelphia fans would boo a funeral. "
Bo Belinsky

" I never questioned the integrity of an umpire. Their eyesight, yes. "
Leo Durocher

" What have they lost, nine of their last eight? "
Ted Turner

" He must have made that before he died. "
Yogi Berra referring to a Steve McQueen movie

" I take a two-hour nap, from one o'clock to four. "
Yogi Berra

Baseball

" After I hit a home run I had a habit of running the bases with my head down. I figured the pitcher already felt bad enough without me showing him up rounding the bases. "
Mickey Mantle

" I gave (pitcher) Mike Cuellar more chances than I gave my first wife. "
Baltimore Orioles manager Earl Weaver

" They say some of my stars drink whiskey. But I have found that the ones who drink milkshakes don't win many ballgames. "
Casey Stengel

" Out of what – a thousand? "
Mickey Rivers on hearing his Yankees teammate Reggie Jackson has an IQ of 165

" Just give me 25 guys on the last year of their contracts; I'll win a pennant every year. "
Sparky Anderson

" People think we make $3 million or $4 million a year. They don't realize that most of us only make $500,000. "
Pete Incaviglia

" I walk into the clubhouse today and it's like walking into the Mayo Clinic. We have four doctors, three therapists and five trainers. Back when I broke in, we had one trainer who carried a bottle of rubbing alcohol, and by the 7th inning he'd already drunk it. "
Tommy Lasorda

" When you get that nice celebration coming into the dugout and you're getting your ass hammered by guys – there's no better feeling than to have that done. "
Matt Stairs

" Two hours is about as long as any American can wait for the close of a baseball game... or anything else for that matter. "
Albert Spalding

" He's got power enough to hit home-runs in any park, including Yellowstone. "
Sparky Anderson on Willie Stargell

" Don't call 'em dogs. Dogs are loyal and they run after balls. "
St. Louis Browns manager Luke Sewell responding to criticism of his team

" There's a thin line between genius and insanity, and in Larry's case it was so thin you could see him drifting back and forth across it. "
Brooklyn Dodgers manager Leo Durocher

Basketball

Players and coaches go through hoops to gain supremacy over each other when they are busy point scoring off court.

Basketball

" We don't need referees in basketball, but
it gives the white guys something to do. "
Charles Barkley

" When I die, I want to come back as me. "
Mark Cuban

" I'm often mentioned in the same sentence as
Michael Jordan. You know 'That Scott Hastings,
he's no Michael Jordan.' "
The self-deprecating Scott Hastings

" Billy Tubbs is what's known as a contact
coach – all con and no tact. "
Bob Reinhardt

" We were so bad last year that the cheerleaders
stayed home and phoned in their cheers. "
Pat Williams

Basketball

" The game is my wife. It demands loyalty and
responsibility and it gives me back fulfilment
and peace. "
Michael Jordan

Reporter: Did you visit the Parthenon
while in Greece?
Basketball star Shaquille O'Neal: I can't really
remember the names of all the clubs we went to.

" I told him, 'Son, what is it with you. Is it
ignorance or apathy?' He said, 'Coach, I don't
know and I don't care.' "
Utah Jazz president Frank Layden

" Left hand, right hand, it doesn't matter.
I'm amphibious. "
Basketball player Charles Shackleford

Basketball

" I've never lost a game. I just ran out of time. "
Michael Jordan

" There are really only two plays: *Romeo and Juliet*, and put the darn ball in the basket. "
Abe Lemons

" The season is too long, the game is too long and the players are too long. "
Jack Dolph

" We can't win at home. We can't win on the road. As general manager, I just can't figure out where else to play. "
Pat Williams

Basketball

" Fans never fall asleep at our games, because they're afraid they might get hit by a pass. "
George Raveling

" In my prime I could have handled Michael Jordan. Of course, he would be only 12 years old. "
Jerry Sloan

" You don't hesitate with Michael, or you'll end up on some poster in a gift shop someplace. "
Fatten Spencer

" Mick Jagger is in better shape than far too many NBA players. It's up in the air whether the same can be said of Keith Richards. "
Bill Walton

" I only know how to play two ways:
reckless and abandon. "
Earvin 'Magic' Johnson

" These are my new shoes. They're good shoes. They
won't make you rich like me, they won't make you
rebound like me, they definitely won't make you
handsome like me. They'll only make you have
shoes like me. That's it. "
Charles Barkley

" It's almost like we have ESPN. "
**Earvin 'Magic' Johnson on his telepathic
understanding with James Worthy**

" If you make every game a life and death
proposition, you're going to have problems.
For one thing, you'll be dead a lot. "
Dean Smith

" Any time Detroit scores more than
100 points and holds the other team
below 100 points, they almost always win. "
Doug Collins

" Nobody roots for Goliath. "
Wilt Chamberlain

" We have a great bunch of outside shooters.
Unfortunately, all our games are played indoors. "
Weldon Drew

" We're going to turn this team around
360 degrees. "
Jason Kidd

Ice Hockey

For a sport that is known for its speed and brutality, surprisingly some of the more vicious moments come when the teams are off the ice.

Ice Hockey

" All hockey players are bi-lingual: they speak
English and profanity."
Gordie Howe

" Hockey is the only game that can be played
equally well with the lights out."
Jim Murray

" A fast body-contact game played by men
with clubs in their hands and knives laced
to their feet."
Paul Gallico

" Goaltending is a normal job, sure. How would
you like it in your job if every time you made a
small mistake, a red light went on over your desk
and 15,000 people stood up and yelled at you."
Jacques Plante

Ice Hockey

" Red ice sells hockey tickets."
Bob Stewart

" If you've only got one day to live,
come see the Toronto Maple Leafs.
It'll seem like forever."
Pat Foley

" I went to a fight the other night and
a hockey game broke out."
Rodney Dangerfield

" By the age of 18, the average American
has witnessed 200,000 acts of violence on
television, most of them occurring during
Game 1 of the NHL playoff series."
Sportswriter Steve Rushin

Ice Hockey

" Half the game is mental; the other half is being mental. "
Jim McKenny

" Hockey is the only job I know where you get paid to have a nap on the day of the game. "
Chico Resch

" Ice hockey is a form of disorderly conduct in which the score is kept. "
Doug Larson

" I know my players don't like my practices, but that's OK because I don't like their games. "
Harry Neale

" I think he knows all my tricks. Or the fact
I don't have any tricks. "
Brendan Shanahan

" They say you're not a coach in the league till
you've been fired. I must be getting pretty good. "
Terry Simpson

" Every day you guys look worse and worse. And
today you played like tomorrow. "
John Mariucci to his US Olympic team

" I don't like hockey. I'm just good at it. "
Brett Hull

" I don't have nightmares about my team. You
gotta sleep before you have nightmares. "
Bep Guidolin, Kansas City Scouts coach

Snooker

Down the years snooker has provided plenty of potty-mouthed moments and more than enough colourful confrontation on the baize as well as off it.

Snooker

" I'm up and down like a whore's drawers. "
**Ronnie O' Sullivan makes a
colourful comparison**

" Jimmy White has popped out to the toilet to
compose himself before the final push. "
Steve Davis getting a bit too close for comfort

" And Griffiths has looked at that blue four times
now, and it still hasn't moved. "
Ted Lowe

" I always have to drink six pints before I'm able to
start playing properly. "
Bill Werbeniuk's meticulous preparation

" I like playing in Sheffield, it's full of
melancholy happy-go-lucky people. "
Alex Higgins

Snooker

" I'll tell you what I would like to do
to Davis. I'd like to stick his cue…"
Alex Higgins

" The audience are literally electrified
and glued to their seats."
Snooker commentator Ted Lowe

" Frankly I would rather have a drink
with Idi Amin."
Alex Higgins on Steve Davis

" This looks like being the longest frame
in the match, even though it's the first."
Clive Everton

" Oh, that's a brilliant shot. The odd thing
is his mum's not very keen on snooker."
Snooker commentator Ted Lowe

" All the reds are in the open apart from the blue."
John Virgo

" Tony Meo is eyeing up a plant."
David Vine

" I don't think it's clever to retire at the top.
I think it's best to go out screaming."
Steve Davis

" 99 times out of 1,000 he would
have potted that ball."
Snooker commentator Ted Lowe

" From this position you've got to fancy either
yourself or your opponent winning."
**Former snooker player and commentator
Kirk Stevens**

Snooker

" If I had to make the choice between staying married and playing snooker, snooker would win. "
Ray Reardon

" I've always said the difference between winning and losing is nothing at all. "
Former snooker player and commentator Terry Griffiths

" Suddenly Alex Higgins is 7–0 down. "
Snooker commentator David Vine

" I don't know if I'm still The Rocket – perhaps I'm more like Thomas the Tank Engine these days. "
Ronnie O'Sullivan

" That's inches away from being millimetre perfect. "
Snooker commentator Ted Lowe

Other Sports

A mixture of mishaps, muck-ups and madness from the saddle and the oche … in boats and on dry land, here is a miscellany of mischief.

" And he's out there in front breaking wind
for the rest of the peloton. "
Phil Liggett on cycling strategy

" Cycling is such a stupid sport. Next time
you are in a car travelling at 40 mph
think about jumping out – naked.
That's what it's like when we crash. "
David Millar

" There are two chairs that will kill you
– the electric chair and the armchair. "
**Former showjumping champion
Harvey Smith on dangers of retirement**

" Well, you gave the horse a wonderful ride
– everybody saw that. "
Television presenter Des Lynam

" The horse sadly died this morning,
so it looks like he won't be running in
the Gold Cup. "
Charlie McCann, trainer

" There are, they say, fools, bloody fools
and men that remount in a steeplechase. "
John Oaksey

" This is really a lovely horse, I once rode
her mother. "
**Race trainer Ted Walsh revealing
training tips**

" This is the first time she has
had 14 hands between her legs. "
John Francombe

" He's been burning the midnight oil
at both ends. "
Darts commentator Sid Waddell

" Only one word for it – magic darts. "
Darts commentator Tony Green

" I can't tell who's leading. It's either
Oxford or Cambridge. "
**John Snagge on the Oxford
and Cambridge boat race**

Other Sports

" Teddy McCarthy to John McCarthy,
no relation, John McCarthy back
to Teddy McCarthy, still no relation..."
**Gaelic football commentator
Micheal O'Muircheartaigh**

" They are unpredictable – horses are
like women."
Jimmy Pike, jockey

" I had him by the bollocks but
I just didn't squeeze."
Phil Taylor

" I thought Aidy was rubbish, and my
rubbish was just a bit better than his."
Gary Anderson, darts player

" The atmosphere is so tense, if Elvis walked in with a portion of chips, you could hear the vinegar sizzle on them. "
Sid Waddell

" The drivers have one foot on the brake, one on the clutch, and one on the throttle. "
Bob Varsha

" Ah, isn't that nice, the wife of the Cambridge president is hugging the cox of the Oxford crew. "
BBC Boat Race commentator

" All I had to do is keep turning left! "
George Robson, winner of the 1946 Indy 500

" You win some, you lose some,
you wreck some. "
Dale Earnhardt Snr

" I feel safer on a racetrack than I do on
Houston's freeways."
AJ Foyt

" And this is Gregorieva from Bulgaria. I saw
her snatch this morning and it was amazing! "
Weightlifting commentator Pat Glenn

Brough Scott: What are your immediate
thoughts, Walter?
Walter Swinburn: I don't have any
immediate thoughts at the moment

Other hilarious football titles from Carlton Books include:

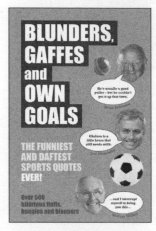

Blunders, Gaffes and Owngoals
ISBN 978-1-78097-586-3

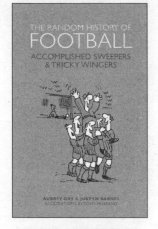

The Random History of Football
ISBN 978-1-85375-936-9

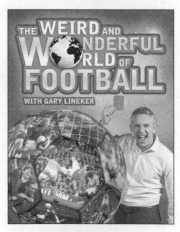

**The Weird and Wonderful
World of Football**
ISBN 978-1-78097-546-7

**The Game of Three Halves:
and Other Bizarre Football Stories**
ISBN 978-1-78097-200-8